Earth-Friendly Buildings, Bridges and More

The Eco-Journal of Corry Lapont

Written by **Etta Kaner**

Illustrated by **Stephen MacEachern**

Kids Can Press

For David, with love and admiration — E.K.
To my family, a strong foundation on which to build — S.M.

Acknowledgments
Thank you to the many people who generously gave of their time, patience and expertise: Mircea Cohn, structural engineer; Rebecca Gaylor, communications manager at Cox Architects and Planners; Miles Moffatt, environmental engineer; Stephen Nelson, Chair of the Department of Earth and Environmental Sciences, Tulane University. A big hug and kiss for Karen Li, my creative editor whose attention to detail and sense of humor is much appreciated. Thank you to Stephen MacEachern for his clever and humorous illustrations and to designer Julia Naimska for her awesome and cool design!

Text © 2012 Etta Kaner
Illustrations © 2012 Stephen MacEachern

Kids Can Press acknowledges the financial support of the Government of Ontario, through the Ontario Media Development Corporation's Ontario Book Initiative; the Ontario Arts Council; the Canada Council for the Arts; and the Government of Canada, through the CBF, for our publishing activity.

Published in Canada by
Kids Can Press Ltd.
25 Dockside Drive
Toronto, ON M5A 0B5

Published in the U.S. by
Kids Can Press Ltd.
2250 Military Road
Tonawanda, NY 14150

www.kidscanpress.com

Edited by Karen Li
Designed by Julia Naimska

This book is smyth sewn casebound.
Manufactured in Malaysia, in 11/2012 by Tien Wah Press (Pte) Ltd.

CM 12 0 9 8 7 6 5 4 3 2

Library and Archives Canada Cataloguing in Publication

Kaner, Etta
    Earth-friendly buildings, bridges and more : the eco-journal of Corry Lapont / written by Etta Kaner ; illustrated by Stephen MacEachern.

Includes index.
ISBN 978-1-55453-570-5

1. Sustainable architecture — Juvenile literature.
2. Urban ecology
(Sociology) — Juvenile literature. I. MacEachern, Stephen II. Title.

Photo credits
Every reasonable effort has been made to trace ownership of and give accurate credit to copyrighted material. Information that would enable the publisher to correct any discrepancies in future editions would be appreciated.
Abbreviations
t = top; b = bottom; c = center; l = left; r = right
p. 7: (l) Clara Kwon, (r) Palabra/Shutterstock.com; p. 16: (c) Clara Kwon, (r) Image courtesy of the City of Melbourne; p. 24: (t) © iStockphoto.com/J. Paul Moore, (b) Hervé Ma; p. 28: (r) Owen Peake; p. 29: (t-l) javarman/Shutterstock.com, (t-r) James R. Hearn/Shutterstock.com; p.30: (b-l) Laitr Keiows/Shutterstock.com, (r) University of Washington Libraries, Special Collections, UW21422; p. 34: (l) Losevsky Pavel/Shutterstock.com, (r) © Guy Montpetit / SODRAC (2011), Archives de la STM (STM Archives); p. 35: (l) D. James Dee, (r) Dimitris Benetos; p. 40: Monolithic Constructors, Inc.; p. 45: (t) Carl Smith, (c) AnnWei/Shutterstock.com, (b) Image courtesy of Georgia Dome; p. 46: (t) © iStockphoto.com/Sebastien Cote, (c) © iStockphoto.com/OnFilm, (b) Photograph © Bob Jones, courtesy Australian Antarctic Division; p. 50: LeonardoG; p. 51: (t) Photo Hydro-Québec; p. 52: Rhys Jones; p. 54: (l) https://beeldbank.rws.nl, Rijkswaterstaat, (r) © iStockphoto.com/OliverChilds; p. 55: (l) www.BeeldbankVenW.nl, Rijkswaterstaat; p. 58, 59: Stephen A. Nelson; p. 60: (l) Shutterstock.com, (t-r) Marco Cannizzaro/Shutterstock.com; p. 61: (l) Luciano Mortula/Shutterstock.com, (r) Steve Speller
All other photos Photos.com/Getty Images

Kids Can Press is a *Corus*™ Entertainment company

CoNTeNtS

Introduction

Hi. I'm Corry Lapont. The book you're holding is my scrapbook. I've been working on it for almost a year. Actually, I've been collecting the postcards of the structures in it for half my life. Sound weird? Mom says it's a case of the apple not falling far from the tree. (Me being the apple, and my parents being the tree.) My parents are both engineers. My mom's a structural engineer, and my dad's an environmental engineer. I guess I get my interest in green (environmentally friendly) structures from my dad.

Ever since I've been little, I've traveled with my parents when they've worked on projects in different parts of the world. That's how I got started on my postcard collection. I've got postcards of spectacular skyscrapers, breathtaking bridges, tremendous tunnels and dazzling domes, as well as incredible dams, dikes, locks and levees.

The upside is that I've actually visited many of these structures and even watched some of them being built! The downside is that my dad insists that I keep a journal of what I'm learning since I miss school when I travel with my parents. (It's not so bad once you get into the habit. Besides, my journal gave me lots of material for this scrapbook.)

Why a scrapbook? Well, it was really my mom's idea. She said it was an excellent way "to put that postcard collection to good use" and "to take advantage of your artistic talent."

How could I refuse? Besides, she bought me a huge scrapbooking kit to sweeten the deal.

Even though I've been working on it for almost a year, you'll see that I'm still not finished. I've got lots of "to-do" notes to myself. So if you've got any suggestions for improvement, I'd love to hear them. Who knows? Once it's perfected, I might even be able to get my scrapbook published!

P.S. On some of the pages, you'll see a boy with red hair and freckles looking a bit like me. That's Riley, my brother, otherwise known as "The Question Box" a.k.a. "The Factoid Finder." Dad "suggested" that I include him in my scrapbook. (It certainly wasn't my idea.) I apologize in advance for his inane questions and comments. Just so you know, they didn't come from me.

Two Ways to Become Famous

1. Stamp collectors are called philatelists. Coin collectors are numismatists. Invent a term for postcard collectors.
2. Get into the Guinness World Records for the greatest number of structures postcards.

SkyScRaPErS

Going Up!

I had a hard time getting up this morning, but I'm sure glad I did! Dad and I took the subway to the Hearst Tower to meet the architect who designed it — Sir Norman Foster. Lord Foster gave us a tour of the tower, which has won several awards for its green design. For example, ninety percent of the steel used to construct the building is recycled.

As soon as we walked into the building, I was blown away. There, right in front of me, was a three-story-high sheet of water flowing next to the escalators!

Hearst Tower

Lord Foster explained that the waterfall, called Icefall, isn't just for show. It helps humidify and cool the lobby. Its water comes from the rainwater collected on the roof. This rainwater is also used to water the plants throughout the building.

Lord Foster pointed out that the building has so much natural light because he designed it with as few inside walls as he could. Then he showed us light sensors that measure the amount of light coming in through the windows and automatically adjust the indoor lights. This cuts down on electricity consumption. No wonder the Hearst Tower won so many awards!

More Cool Skyscrapers

Torre Agbar
Barcelona, Spain

- Solar cells on its outer walls generate electricity for the building.
- Its windows tilt to block out direct sunlight and keep the building cool.

> The Torre Agbar has 4400 windows!

> I'm glad I'm not the window washer!

One Bryant Park
New York City, U.S.

- It uses rainwater and recycled wash water for toilets and landscaping.
- Tanks in the basement make giant ice cubes that cool the building as they melt.

Check This Out

Why do skyscrapers have broad bases? Lord Foster said to try this: Stand with your feet together and have a friend try to push you over from the side. Then stand with your feet apart and ask your friend to try to push you over again. (I'll ask my friend David to help me and see what happens.)

Checking Out the Site

Dad says that building any kind of skyscraper (green or not) will have an impact on the environment. That's why a lot of planning and teamwork are involved before you even put a shovel in the ground. It was so cool to meet the different kinds of engineers and architects on the planning team and hear about their jobs. I got some good ideas of what I could become!

Architect
I design the building so that it meets the needs of its users and respects the surrounding neighborhood. I investigate the shadow that the skyscraper would cast on nearby buildings. For example, it might shade solar panels and make them less efficient. We use computer programs to figure this out.

Urban planner
I make sure that the planned building follows the city's planning rules. The rules control the height of a building, its shape and its use — whether the building will be for apartments or offices or stores.

Civil engineer
I make sure that the building can connect to the city's water and sewage pipes. I help design the driveway and parking lot to make sure that rainwater does not pollute or flood the neighborhood's pipes.

Structural engineer
Building a skyscraper among existing skyscrapers can change the way the wind flows. I measure how a new wind load — wind pressure — will affect surrounding buildings.

Geotechnical engineer
Checking what's underground is just as important as checking what's on the surface. Often there are several feet of water underground. Engineers need to know how much water there is so that they can plan for draining it. We also check the soil to decide what kind of foundation to build.

Transportation engineer
My job is to find out how many people will be working in the skyscraper, and how many will be using public transportation at what times of the day. Then we will know if more buses or subway cars are needed and on which routes. We also need to plan for bicycle racks and parking.

Getting to the Bottom of Things

They just finished digging the foundation for a skyscraper across the street from our apartment. The building will probably be very tall because the foundation hole looks really deep. (Mom says that a foundation must be deep enough to support the weight of the building.) After I'd done a lot of urging (i.e., nagging), Mom introduced me to the site manager so that I could get a closer look. Workers were building the supports for the skyscraper when we got there.

In the bottom of the foundation hole were these huge concrete blocks called footings. Each footing had a large steel column attached to it. The footings and columns support the skyscraper — if the ground is solid.

"So what if it's not solid?" I asked Ms. Gomez, the site manager. She explained that engineers can use two other kinds of foundation supports to ensure that a building will be stable.

Me wearing my designer (by moi!) hard hat with Ms. Gomez.

"When the ground is a mixture of sand and water, it's very weak. A giant hollow concrete box, called a raft, is used to support the columns. The raft floats in the wet soil. When the ground is weak but not wet, long steel posts called piles are hammered into it. The piles are driven into the ground until they reach solid soil or rock. Footings are then placed on top of the piles."

> Do you know that Shanghai has so many skyscrapers that its soft soil is sinking under their weight?

> Talk about getting that sinking feeling!

One Way to Become Famous

I've invented an experiment that will answer Riley's question (which is not bad for once), "How do engineers know what kind of soil they'll be building on?"

- Make a tower of three blocks of modeling clay, each block a different color.
- Carefully screw a corkscrew (with Mom or Dad's permission) down through all three layers.
- Gently pull the corkscrew up and out.

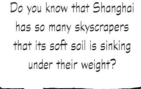

Geotechnical engineers do a similar thing to test the soil. They dig deep into the soil with a corkscrew-like machine called a drilling rig. The drilling rig brings up soil samples from different depths just like the corkscrew brings up three colors of clay.

Give Me Strength!

This is me working on the core of 340 on the Park in Chicago, U.S. (just kidding). The core is a vertical (up and down) tube that helps support a high-rise. As well as giving a building strength, this is where the elevators, emergency stairs, air ducts, water pipes and electrical wires go.

Mom says that to build a strong core, engineers use steel and sometimes reinforced concrete (concrete with steel rods running through it). The core often has steel cross-bracing (large Xs) to give it strength.

Engineers also use steel to build the skeleton frame of a high-rise. The frame is made of vertical columns and horizontal beams that reach across from one column to another. When you look at a column or beam from its end, it looks like a capital letter I. That's why it's called an I-beam. This shape helps make the columns, beams and skeleton frame strong enough to support the weight of the building.

The condo 340 on the Park is really awesome. Each side has a different shape, with the east end pointed like the prow of a ship. I wish we could live in it!

The building has all kinds of green features, like bamboo floors, kitchen counters made of recycled materials, energy-efficient lights, dual-flush toilets and a 41 600 L (11 000 gal.) tank in the basement for storing rainwater. The rainwater is used for watering the rooftop garden and the two-story winter garden. It also reduces the amount of water run-off into the storm sewers.

Are you looking for a strong, sustainable material for your floors? Use bamboo. It grows back very quickly after it's been cut.

Save water with a dual-flush toilet! It uses only 3 L (0.8 gal.) for liquid waste and 6 L (1.6 gal.) for solid waste.

Check This Out

Some skyscrapers have cross-bracing on their core and on their cladding (outside) to make them strong. Why do engineers use cross-bracing for strength? As usual, Mom told me to find out for myself.

- Get seven straws and six pipe cleaners.
- Cut five straws in half and discard one of the halves.
- Leave two straws whole.
- Cut the pipe cleaners in half and discard one of the halves. Use them with the straws to make a square, rectangle and triangle.
- Lay the three shapes on a table and push on their sides.

The winner is the shape that doesn't move! Using a shape that is stable gives a building strength. The cross-bracing formed by large Xs on buildings is made up of triangles.

Skyscrapers Beware!

Am I ever glad to be home! I never thought when we left home that I'd be in the middle of not one, but two earth-shaking and mind-blowing experiences.

The first one happened in Mexico City, Mexico. Dad and I were approaching the Torre Mayor skyscraper where we were going to take a tour. Suddenly, I was jolted off balance (like when you're standing in the aisle of a bus, and it brakes sharply). I saw parked cars and trees shaking like crazy. Dad and I ran inside the Torre Mayor. It was like we had entered another time zone. Everything was still, and the office people were working as if nothing were wrong.

Our tour guide, Señor Garcia, welcomed us with a smile. He explained that the Torre Mayor has so many earthquake-resistant features that earthquakes, which are common in Mexico City, are rarely felt inside the building.

Señor Garcia said that many earthquake-resistant skyscrapers use base isolators to lessen the impact of earthquakes. Often these are giant pads made of alternating layers of rubber and steel plates. They separate a structure from the ground so that an earthquake's vibrations have less effect on the building.

Torre Mayor

- Two hundred and fifty-two piles have been driven into bedrock 60 m (200 ft.) below the building.

- The core is built with reinforced concrete and steel as well as trusses (triangles of steel).

- Steel rods in reinforced concrete allow the concrete to bend a bit without breaking.

- The steel frame has 98 dampers — long tubes filled with fluid that absorb the energy of the earthquake. This reduces the amount of energy that enters the columns and beams.

My mind-blowing experience was really a wind-blowing experience. Dad and I were touring the tuned mass damper in the Taipei 101 skyscraper in Taipei, Taiwan. A tuned mass damper (TMD) is a huge weight that reduces the swaying of a building in high winds. On many buildings, a TMD is a giant concrete block attached to the sides of the flat roof with springs. When a strong wind pushes the building in one direction, the TMD slides in the opposite direction. The weight of the TMD prevents the building from swaying too much.

Did you know that the Taipei 101 TMD is the biggest in the world? It weighs 660 tonnes (730 tons). That's the weight of forty-four city buses!

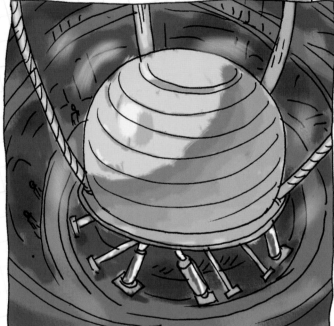

Taipei 101

The TMD in Taipei 101 is different. It's a giant steel sphere that hangs from the ninety-second floor in an open circular space. As we stood on the observation walkway looking at the TMD and the cables that supported it, I started to feel a little dizzy. Then I realized that the TMD was moving. Dad said that if we could actually see it move, there must be a huge wind load on the building. He was right! We were in the middle of a typhoon! Luckily, we were able to stay in Taipei 101 until the typhoon was over.

Listen to this! The swimming pool on the fifty-seventh floor of the Jin Mao Tower in China acts as a damper.

I wonder how much water it takes to dampen (get it?) the building's movement.

Green Hall of Fame

I hereby declare that the following high-rises have been nominated for Corry's Green High-Rise Hall of Fame. Each building will be awarded an esteemed Corry certificate for environmentally friendly design.

Swiss Re
London, England

This building is commonly known as the Gherkin because of its pickle-like shape. One of its many green features is that it has no private car parking spaces. But it has lots of parking for bicycles!

Condé Nast
New York, U.S.

This office tower is nicknamed the Green Giant for its many Earth-friendly features. One of them is that the building does not need to be heated or cooled for most of the year, thanks to its unique outer walls.

Council House 2
Melbourne, Australia

One of the many green features of this unusual building is its air quality. Every half hour, there is a one hundred percent change of fresh air.

BRiDgEs

Building Bridges

Ms. Corry Lapont
1475 Meadowwood Street
Vancouver
B.C.

Dear Ms. Lapont,
The Alberta Ministry of Transportation would like you to build a bridge over the Blow River. Please let us know what kind of bridge you intend to build — beam, arch, cantilever, suspension, movable — and what it will cost. Thank you.

Sincerely,

Tran Sporter

Mr. Tran Sporter

ARCH

BEAM

SUSPENSION

MOVABLE

CANTILEVER

Dear Mr. Sporter,
Thank you for asking me to build your bridge. Before I can determine the most appropriate kind of bridge and its cost, I need to find answers to the following questions:
1. What distance will the bridge span (cross over)?
2. What will the live load (traffic, people, wind, rain, changes in temperature) be on the bridge?
3. What is the dynamic load (sudden strong winds, earthquakes)?
4. What kind of boat traffic will there be?
5. What kind of soil is on the bottom and the banks of the river?
6. How deep is the water, and how strong is its current?
7. What kinds of building materials are available?
8. What is the ecosystem (natural environment) in the area?

My team and I will research this information and get back to you as soon as possible.

Sincerely,

Corry Lapont

Ms. Corry Lapont

Hey, these aren't real letters!

I know. I'm just practicing in case I become an engineer.

Beam Bridges

I'm still "beaming" about the beam bridge Dad and I visited today! Like many beam bridges, the Tsable River Bridge was constructed with a box girder — a long, hollow, concrete box under the deck, or roadway. (Dad says that box girders make a bridge strong because of their shape and stiffness. He says that beam bridges can also be built with I-beams, but box girders are usually used for spanning longer distances.)

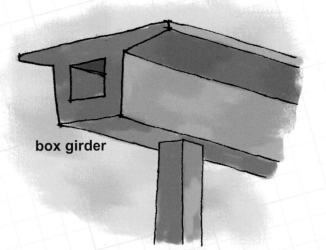

box girder

What's so amazing about this bridge is that it spans a river valley full of Douglas firs so old that many of them reach up past the bridge. The river valley is filled with wildlife — black bears, cougars, black-tailed deer, bald eagles, blue herons and lots of different species of fish. To minimize the impact of the

bridge on the animals' ecosystem, engineers built the Tsable River Bridge with only three piers (bridge supports). The middle pier was built on an island in the river to protect the fish habitat. No wonder this bridge won not only one, but two awards of excellence!

While we were looking at the bridge, we met an engineer who built two beam bridges out of 95 tonnes (100 tons) of recycled plastic. (That's equal to 1.4 million one-gallon milk jugs!) These bridges in Fort Bragg, U.S., are strong enough to support a tank. Apparently, plastic bridges have a lot of advantages.

They don't need to be painted to prevent rusting. Plus they are lighter, cheaper and use less energy to produce than steel or wood bridges. Since they corrode (wear away) very slowly and resist rot and damaging insects, they probably won't need to be repaired or replaced as often.

Dad and the engineer had a lot in common. They both build with the environment in mind. The engineer said that if we really want to get serious about recycling materials, we should use them in building large structures. Hmm … I wonder what you could build out of recycled paper?

> Did you see any animal bridges like they have in Europe? They build wide bridges over highways and plant them with grass, bushes and trees. Animals use them to get from one side of the highway to the other.

> They have them in North America, too. They're called ecopassages. We even have them under highways for burrowing animals like badgers and foxes, and for amphibians.

Check This Out

Mom says that since the weight of a bridge and its traffic loading all press down on a bridge's piers, the piers must support a lot of compression. She challenged me to find the strongest pier shape to use for a bridge.

- Make three columns — a cylinder, a square shape and a triangular shape — out of three sheets of paper and clear tape. Make sure the columns are the same height, and use the same amount of tape for each.
- Pile paperback books one at a time on each column. Which supports the most books?

21

Truss and Cantilever Bridges

I grumbled while working on this project, but these parts were definitely worth saving!

Truss and Cantilever Bridges *by Corry Lapont*

Truss bridges are beam bridges strengthened by trusses — a series of triangles made of steel. The trusses ensure the strength and rigidity of the beam by dissipating (spreading out) the load. Trusses are used on railway bridges to support the weight and vibrations of trains. They are also used to strengthen the deck of suspension bridges and to support some movable bridges.

The triangles in a truss bridge can be organized into many different patterns. These patterns are named after the people who invented them.

A cantilever bridge is a type of truss bridge. It is built over a body of water where a longer span and wider clearance for boats is needed.

A cantilever bridge usually consists of two piers with cantilever arms extending horizontally from the sides of each pier (like your arms held straight out from your body). The cantilevers are supported by a truss framework. Often there is a span or deck between the cantilevers to make the bridge longer.

Why Are Triangles Strong?

Triangles are strong because they cannot be pushed out of shape like other polygons. In fact, to strengthen a polygon like a rectangle or a square, supports can be added to form triangles within the shapes.

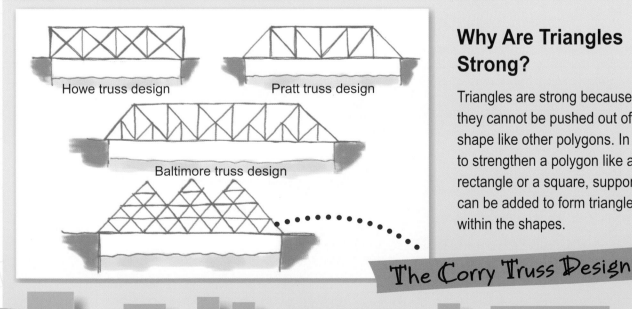

Howe truss design

Pratt truss design

Baltimore truss design

The Corry Truss Design

Compression and Tension

All bridges experience compression (squeezing) or tension (stretching) or both. To understand how this works, I did the following:

- I got a sponge 13 cm (5 in.) long.
- With a marker, I drew vertical lines 2 cm (¾ in.) apart along the long side of the sponge.
- I rested the ends of the sponge on two thick books to make a bridge.
- I put a can of tuna on the sponge.

At the top of the sponge, the spaces between the lines were squeezed together (in compression), and at the bottom, the spaces were wider apart (in tension).

Scotland

One of the strongest cantilever bridges ever built is the Forth Railway Bridge in Scotland. It was the first bridge in Britain to be built out of steel. It is used by both passenger and freight trains.

Canada

The Quebec Bridge is the longest cantilever bridge in the world. It took twenty years to plan and construct this steel bridge. It is used by pedestrians, cyclists, cars and trains.

Arch Bridges

Welcome to the World's First Annual Arch Bridge Design Exhibition. I am your host architect, Corry Lapont. I am pleased to say that our tour includes an exciting display of arch bridge designs. But first, a little background information. Arch bridges are built over roads, rivers and steep valleys. Since the arch shape is naturally strong, arch bridges don't need to be supported by piers, which block the passage of boats on a busy river. Instead, they are supported by abutments — heavy concrete blocks or natural rock — at either end. Now let's begin our tour. I'll be happy to answer any questions along the way.

Natchez Trace Parkway Bridge
Tennessee, U.S.
Concrete arch bridge

The two arches of this bridge are unique because they were built without spandrels (columns connecting the deck to the arch). I think you'll agree that this makes the bridge look more open and pleasing to the eye.

La Coulée Verte
Paris, France
Stone arch bridge

Speaking of being pleasing to the eye, this bridge was built in 1858 as an elevated railway. Instead of demolishing the bridge when it closed in 1969, the city built a 4 km (2½ mi.) garden along its top. Turning this bridge into a garden helped reduce air pollution and avoided creating demolition garbage.

New River Gorge Bridge

Fayetteville, U.S.

Deck above steel arch bridge

When this bridge was completed, driving time across the gorge was cut from forty-five minutes to forty-five seconds because people no longer had to take a long detour around the gorge. To support the weight of the arch and traffic loading, engineers used steel. The rocky sides of the gorge were used as the bridge's abutments.

A-*but*-ments? You're kidding. Did you just make that up?

I'll show you what I mean.

Check This Out

An arch bridge is naturally strong because of its shape. But it still needs abutments at the ends of the bridge to support it. They might be the rocky sides of a gorge or heavy concrete blocks. Try this out to see how they work:

- Cut a 1 cm (1/4 in.) strip off the end of an empty toilet paper roll.
- Make one cut in the strip to form an arch.
- Stand the arch on a table and press down on the top.
- Now put books at both ends of the arch and press down on it.

The books act as abutments. An arch bridge is always under compression. The force of the compression goes into the abutments. The abutments push back on the arch and give it support.

Suspension Bridges

This is the best trip ever! I actually walked across nine suspension bridges — the Golden Gate Bridge in San Francisco, U.S., and eight others right here in Vancouver! I'm really glad that I got these pamphlets because I could never remember everything our tour guides told us (even though I was "hanging" on every word they said).

Welcome to the Golden Gate Bridge, the most-photographed bridge in the world. Please use this pamphlet to take a self-guided tour. We hope you enjoy your visit.

Like all suspension bridges, the Golden Gate Bridge was built in three stages: the towers, the anchorages and the cables.

The Towers

The two towers were built out of reinforced concrete. The pier of one of the towers was built on bedrock not far below the surface of the water. The other pier was much more challenging. It was built 34 m (110 ft.) below the surface. To do this, a hollow cofferdam (a box as big as a football field) was lowered to the ocean floor. The cofferdam was filled with a special concrete that hardens under water. After the concrete hardened, the cofferdam was removed and the tower was built on top of the pier.

The Anchorages

The anchorages are the giant concrete blocks at either end of the bridge. The ends of the cables are embedded in these blocks. The anchorages must be heavy enough to support the cables, the roadway and the traffic on it. That's why each anchorage weighs 54 400 tonnes (60 000 tons)!

The Cables

The thick cables that you see draped over the tops of the towers are made up of thousands of pencil-thick steel wires. To make a cable, a large wheel spins individual wires from one anchorage to the other, over the towers and across the bridge. When there are enough wires to create a thick bundle (about 1 m, or 3 ft., across), the wires are wrapped with more steel to make a single cable. It took over six months to spin the wires for this bridge!

The cables have enough wire to go around the world three times. And the towers are as tall as a seventy-four-story skyscraper!

Check This Out

Why does a suspension bridge need anchorages? Our tour guide told us to try this when we got home:

- Stand two chairs back-to-back, 65 cm (26 in.) apart. These are the towers of a suspension bridge.
- Tie a length of string from the top of one chair to the top of the other so that the string forms a shallow curve.
- Tie another string in the same way beside the first one. Then slide the strings as far apart as possible.
- Press down on the two strings. What happens to the chairs?
- Use more string and heavy books to stop the chairs from caving in.

They were so right when they called this the thrill of a lifetime! We started out wobbling our way across the steel Capilano Suspension Bridge in Vancouver. I held my breath as I concentrated on putting one foot in front of the other. My stomach did flip-flops when I looked down at the Capilano River flowing over boulders twenty-three storys below us. But I made it across! With my adrenalin pumping, I was ready for the suspension bridges of the Treetops Adventure. These seven bridges aren't as long or as high as the Capilano Bridge, but it was still cool to walk 30 m (100 ft.) above the forest floor. We walked among the tops of spruce, cedar and hemlock, but to see the tops of the Douglas firs, we really had to strain our necks. They were tree-mendous. As we stood on one of the viewing platforms that link the bridges from one Douglas fir to another, we could see Grandma Capilano,

the tallest tree in the forest. What was really awesome was that none of these trees were harmed during the construction of the platforms and the bridges!

Get the thrill of a lifetime!

Cross the Capilano Canyon on the Capilano Suspension Bridge. Then go on an amazing rain forest Treetops Adventure!

On the Move

I love watching movable bridges! I'm always surprised when I see what looks like a permanent structure suddenly spring to life. Mom says that movable bridges are usually built over waterways where it's too difficult or too expensive to build a bridge high enough for ships to pass under. Movable bridges like swing bridges are sometimes built near airports because they have no towers to interfere with air traffic. Others are built in places where there is much more boat traffic than car and pedestrian traffic. If I were an engineer, I would choose to build a movable bridge just because they're so much fun.

Tilting bridge
The Gateshead Millennium Bridge is sooo cool! It was built for pedestrians and cyclists, and it's the only tilting bridge in the world. When it tilts to let small ships pass, its reflection looks like a huge eye opening up. No wonder its nickname is the Blinking Eye Bridge.

Swing bridge
The Sale Swing Bridge was built in 1883 and is still operating! (It was renovated in 2006.) The deck rotates on its pier to let boats pass through one of the channels on either side of the pier.

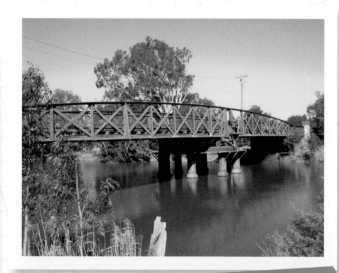

Latrobe River, Australia

River Tyne, England

Transporter bridge (a.k.a. ferry bridge)

Whoever invented the Vizcaya Bridge was a genius! It transports people and cars on a gondola (hanging platform) from one bank of a river to the other without interrupting river traffic. This gondola can transport six cars and several dozen people in just one-and-a-half minutes.

Nervión River, Spain

Vertical lift bridge

When a ship needs to pass under the Hawthorne Bridge, one of its spans lifts straight up. The operator in the control room explained that it works like an elevator with pulleys, long steel cables, a small electric motor and a 400 tonne (450 ton) concrete counterweight in each tower. In addition to lifting and lowering the span, the operator is also in charge of all the lights and gates that control traffic.

Willamette River, U.S.

Double-leaf bascule bridge

We were really lucky to see the Tower Bridge open because it only opens four or five times a week. We also got to see the massive engines in the towers that lift the two 450 kg (1000 lb.) bascules (decks). Amazingly, the raising of the bascules only takes about a minute.

Thames River, England

Listen to this! In 1952, the driver of a bus was near the edge of the south bascule of the Tower Bridge when the bridge started to open. He sped up the bus, and it was able to jump the gap! And no one was really hurt.

Bridges Under Attack!

Confederation Bridge

This beam bridge's biggest problem is ice. So engineers designed a large cone at the base of each pier. Ice floes break when they ride up the cones.

Northumberland Strait, Canada

Akashi-Kaikyo Bridge

This suspension bridge has to withstand both earthquakes and typhoons! Each tower was built with twenty tuned mass dampers inside.

Akashi Strait, Japan

Tacoma Narrows Bridge

In 1940, wind caused this suspension bridge to collapse. But the wind wasn't very strong. The problem was the way the bridge was constructed. The deck was very narrow compared to its length, which allowed torsion (twisting by the wind). Also, the sides were solid, which gave the wind a surface to push against. When engineers rebuilt the bridge, they widened the deck and put open trusses under the deck to strengthen it. The wind could blow through the triangles instead of pushing against the sides of the bridge.

Puget Sound, U.S.

TunNeLs

31

Tunnels

Tunneling is such boring work.

I wish Mr. Fischer weren't so strict. All I did was giggle while he was teaching, and he punishes me with an essay about tunnels. I wasn't even laughing at him. I just thought my cartoon doodle was funny. It was even on topic. At least I got a good mark after all the research I did.

Corry Lapont
Mr. Fischer/Science 6
February 10, 2010

Tunnels and the Environment

People build tunnels for many reasons. One of the main reasons is for transportation. Tunnels built through hills or mountains cut down traveling time. Instead of going up and then down a slope, drivers just go straight through. Drivers are also protected from rain, snow and ice.

Tunnels built under cities also reduce traveling time. Cars can travel at a higher speed without having to make their way through city streets — a lot like traveling on a highway. When traffic is directed underground, the surface can be used for other purposes like buildings, parks, bicycle paths and pedestrian walkways.

Tunnels also carry subways as well as pipes for fresh water, sewage, oil, natural gas and cables.

Before choosing a route for an underground tunnel, engineers investigate the effect of the tunnel-building project on the environment. Some of the biggest impacts on the environment are from the shafts (wide vertical tunnels) that are built first. Usually, three shafts are built per tunnel — one for removing the muck (soil and rock), one for moving equipment in and out, and one for ventilation. Engineers research the answers to such questions as:

- How will drilling the shafts affect nearby buildings?
- Will the drilling uncover any artifacts?
- Will the shafts affect any animal habitats?
- Will the shafts cause erosion of soil into nearby streams?
- Will the shafts hit groundwater?
- Will building the shafts cause a lot of noise pollution to nearby residents?
- How will getting the muck out of the area affect the environment?

Once engineers know where they're going to build the tunnel, geotechnical engineers drill deep into the earth to bring up many core samples. The core samples tell them the type of soil or bedrock the tunnel will go through. The samples also show whether there are metals, water, hazardous wastes or fissures (cracks) in the ground.

Building a tunnel definitely affects the environment. But engineers study the possible impacts on the environment and try to lessen them.

Did you know that subway engineers in Rome, Italy, keep finding all kinds of old stuff when they dig? They've found parts of a palace, a kitchen, a copper factory and even human skeletons!

I think they call that old "stuff" artifacts.

Subways
(Not the Eating Kind!)

I should never have let Dad see my postcards of super-cool subway art. He insisted on taking me to the building site of the new subway line near his work. I told him it was the artwork that interested me, but he said that I should "never miss a learning opportunity." Well, I did learn a lot. (Maybe it'll come in handy for a school project. I'd better write it down before I forget.)

Subways are often built by the cut and cover method. The first thing workers do is place steel piles deep into the earth around the perimeter of the trench that they're going to dig. They place wooden walls between the piles to stop earth from caving in. Then machines like bulldozers, backhoes and front-end loaders dig a deep trench in the earth. Construction workers build a steel or wooden form (mold) in the trench for the top, bottom and sides of the tunnel. They fill the form with reinforced concrete, often embedding pipes for cables, wires and water in the concrete. Once the concrete hardens, they remove the form. After the tunnel is built, the trench is filled with soil and a new road is built above.

Komsomolskaya
subway station

I love the marble walls and chandeliers in this subway station in Moscow, Russia. It looks like a palace.

Assomption
subway station

Artist Guy Montpetit is a "guy" after my own heart. I love the bright colors he used on this subway corridor in Montreal, Canada. I bet that by the time you reach the end in the morning, you're totally awake.

14th Street
subway station

Artist Tom Otterness has a crazy sense of humor. This bronze sculpture in the New York City subway is one of more than one hundred pieces in a collection called "Life Underground."

Ethniki Amyna
subway station

Artist Kostas Tsoklis calls this artwork in the Athens, Greece, subway station "Underground Park." It looks more like a forest to me!

Two Ways to Become Famous

1. Design a totally awesome mosaic for our new subway line.
2. Create more ways for subway systems to be environmentally friendly like these:

- Use low-energy lights.
- Use collected rainwater to wash subway trains.
- Use skylights in subway stations to cut down the amount of artificial light needed.
- Use solar power.
- Recycle materials during construction or expansion.
- Save energy by not heating or cooling tunnels or stations.

More Tunneling —
This Time with TBMs

When a tunnel must travel deeper (as under buildings or waterways), it is dug with a tunnel boring machine (TBM).

TBMs are also used to tunnel through mountains. These machines are enormous! They can be as long as four football fields laid end to end and as tall as a five-story building. The front of the TBM is like a giant tin can with a huge cutting wheel at its front. When the TBM pushes forward, the cutting wheel rotates and grinds down the rock. The chewed up rock falls through spaces in the wheel onto a conveyor belt, which carries it to rail cars on a track inside the tunnel. The rail cars carry the muck out of the mountain.

TBMs build supports for the tunnel walls at the same time as they bore the tunnel. A machine behind the cutting wheel places either steel mesh or steel rings along the tunnel walls. Then a robot sprays shotcrete (sticky concrete) from a hose onto the steel supports to line the tunnel.

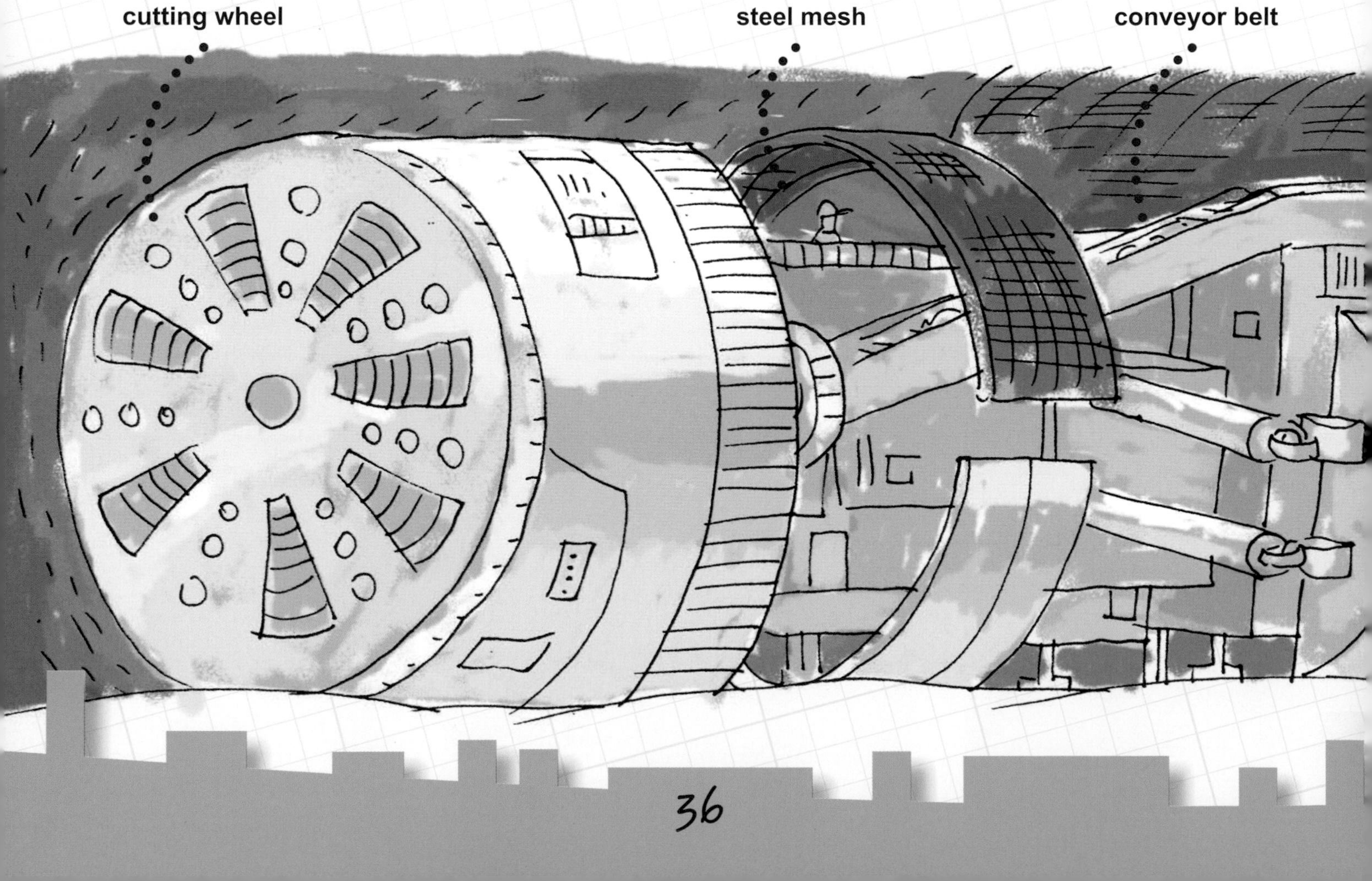

cutting wheel

steel mesh

conveyor belt

Listen to this! Naked mole rats work like TBMs. To tunnel through hard soil they line up. The first mole rat digs with his claws and kicks the dirt back to the animal behind it. The dirt is passed down the line to the outside of the burrow.

I'll bet that's where the inventors of TBMs got their idea.

Check This Out

I didn't get to see a working TBM, so Dad said he would help me try this:

- Cut four rectangular holes from the bottom of a plastic margarine container.
- With a nail, punch three holes between each rectangular hole. Punch the holes from the inside of the container toward the outside.
- Dig a hole in some hard earth so that the container can fit into it.
- Place the container on its side in the hole with the bottom against the earth. Push against the earth while turning the container back and forth.

shotcrete robot

DomEs

Dome Sweet Dome

640 East 5th Avenue
Tallahassee, Florida

January 21, 2010

Dear Corry,

I couldn't find any dome postcards for your scrapbook, so I'm sending you a photo instead. This is a vacation house we rented a few years ago in Pensocola Beach, Florida. The home's owners had it built after tropical storms destroyed their previous house. I know it looks weird, but it's amazing to stay in. You would love it — especially because it's so green.

This dome home uses much less energy for heating and cooling than your house because it has no corners to trap and waste warmed or cooled air. This also means that the air circulation is more even. The dome shape uses less building material than a house with straight walls.

You might think there is less indoor space than a conventional house, but it's just the opposite. It actually has more room than a square or rectangular house built with the same amount of material! If you don't believe me, try the attached experiment.

Most important of all, the building is virtually tornado proof, hurricane proof and even earthquake proof. Wind blows around the house instead of hitting a flat wall and knocking it down. This dome home has already survived Hurricanes Ivan, Dennis and Katrina!

Our vacation home was also powered by geothermal energy. Do you know about that? If not, here's how it works. Pipes filled with fluid are laid below the surface of the ground and connected to a building. In winter, natural heat from the ground transfers to the fluid in the pipes. The heat from the fluid goes into your house to keep you warm. In the summer, heat from your house goes back into the fluid, which cools the house down. A geothermal system is Earth friendly and doesn't create pollution like gas or oil or coal.

I probably sound like an ad for domes, but they really are awesome. You should come down and see some (and us, too, of course!). Say hi to Riley and your parents for me.

Your cousin,

Michael

Michael

15°C
(60°F)
all year
round

Check This Out

To prove that dome homes have more space inside than a square or rectangular home, Michael told me to try this:

- Take three long pipe cleaners of equal length. Bend one into a circle, another into a rectangle and the third into a square. Twist the ends to hold the shapes.
- Place marbles (all the same size) in the circle to fill it with a single layer.
- Count the number of marbles in the circle.
- Use the same marbles to fill the rectangle and the square.
- Which shape holds the most marbles?

41

The Geodesic Dome

We just got back to our hotel from the Biosphere, a totally cool environment museum here in Montreal, Canada. The visit would have been perfect if Ms. Bryant hadn't yelled at me (in front of the whole class) for getting lost. I wasn't lost. I knew where I was. I'd just stayed behind to re-watch the film about Buckminster Fuller, the guy who designed the Biosphere. He was really awesome. He devoted his life to eliminating world poverty and hunger. He believed that his geodesic dome design could solve the world's housing shortage.

Sam, Michelle, David and me (Corry) in front of the Biosphere

Geodesic domes use triangles, so they are strong and stable. They are easy and quick to build and relatively inexpensive. They also save energy and use a minimum amount of material. The weird thing is that a geodesic dome is the only structure that gets stronger as it gets larger. That's because more triangles share the load and make the dome rounder.

There were a lot of cool things at the Biosphere aside from the Buckminster movie: I really loved the museum's e*coo*logical solar-powered house. I walked on water in the Water Wonders section. I watched a presentation called X-Treme Weather. (Talk about scary!) I climbed the wall in the Moving Giant exhibition, and I even made a sculpture out of recycled materials!

I can't wait to get back home, though. Our class is going to participate in the Biosphere's Agent X Project. We each get a special Agent X identity card. Our mission is to infiltrate our home and school environment and make our family and friends more eco-aware. I hope I get to design my own sunglasses!

> You know, animals build dome homes, too.

> Yeah. A beaver builds its lodge out of mud and sticks. A soldier crab makes an igloo out of sand. And a filmy dome spider spins a silk web that looks like an upside-down bowl.

Check This Out

Be on the first team to build a geodesic dome big enough to hold one person. This was our class challenge. Our teacher suggested that we use struts of rolled up newspaper to form the dome's triangles. She said to

- Use a pile of three or four sheets of newspaper for each strut.
- Start rolling the papers from a corner.
- Start rolling the papers with a pencil to make sure the roll is tight.
- Cut off the uneven ends of each roll and staple the ends closed.
- Connect the struts with tape or staples.

> We did it. Our team rocks!

Under the Big Dome

Riley drove me CRAZY today! It was the fourth inning at Rogers Centre, and the Toronto Blue Jays were leading. Suddenly, the domed roof started to close. (I guess it looked like rain.) Instead of watching the game, Riley started tugging on my sleeve and giving me a blow-by-blow description of the roof closing. (Yeah, it was interesting, but I'd seen it before.) "Look, Corry, one of the panels is sliding around the rim of the stadium. Now the other two are moving across to join the first one. Look up there. The roof is full of triangles."

Then Riley started in with the questions. "Do all stadiums have roofs? Are stadiums used only for sports events?"

Luckily, Mom is the patient one in the family. She explained that many stadiums don't have roofs, but the ones that do are usually dome shaped. Domes are strong and can be supported without columns, which would block the view of the playing field. Then Mom said that stadiums are also used for concerts, operas, races and special events like monster truck shows.

Rogers Centre

Check This Out

Dad said to try this eggs-periment to show how strong the dome shape is. He said to

- Interlock my fingers to make a cup shape.
- Ask Riley to place an uncooked egg into the cup.
- Squeeze hard on both ends of the egg with the palms of my hands.

Dad says that it's impossible to break the egg. We'll try it and see if he is eggs-aggerating.

Awesome Stadium Domes

AAMI Park
Melbourne, Australia

The roof of this stadium is really made of twenty attached roofs! Each roof is a cantilever in the shape of a geodesic dome, which gives the roof its strength. The stadium's water is solar heated and it harvests rainwater to use for flushing toilets and washing the stands.

Sapporo Dome
Sapporo City, Japan

The roof of the Sapporo Dome doesn't move, but its field does! When games switch from baseball to soccer, the turf is rolled up. The huge doors open and a gigantic natural grass soccer pitch is rolled in from outside. The pitch moves on wheels and a cushion of air pressure, hovering 7.5 cm (3 in.) above the ground.

Georgia Dome
Atlanta, U.S.

The Georgia Dome's roof is supported like an open umbrella. Its fiberglass fabric stretches over a frame of steel triangles. The dome has lots of green features. It recycles pop cans, plastic, paper, glass and water. It composts food waste and donates food to food banks.

All Roads Lead to Dome

Canada
Home
Antarctica
United King

Quebec City, Canada

Here's a really "cool" dome! The Ice Hotel near Quebec City, Canada, is only open for three months each year since it melts in the spring. Everything is made of ice or snow — even the beds.

St. Austell, United Kingdom

Eden Project is a series of domes built to teach people about the environment. The domes were built with steel frames covered with huge "pillows" of strong material filled with air. The air insulates the domes in cold weather.

Antarctica

These apple huts are made of fiberglass and can be quickly built by two people. Many Australian scientists live in them when they work in the Antarctic.

DamS, DikES, LoCKs, LEvEEs

Dams

I don't get it. Why are dams so tall and reservoirs so huge?

It's lucky I've got lots of dam postcards. I'll be able to use them during the debate on dams in science class. The only problem is that Mr. Evans refuses to tell me which side I'll be on — pro or con. He says that it's important "to be informed about both sides of an issue." Personally, I think that becoming informed about both sides just means double the amount of work (groan). But I guess I should understand the basics, like how a dam is built and how it works.

Dam
A dam is a high, wide wall built across a river to block its water flow. (Some dams are as tall as a ninety-eight-story skyscraper!) Dams are built in river valleys. The valley might be a narrow canyon or wide and flat.

Penstocks
Penstocks are tunnels inside the dam. (Some are as wide as my classroom!) Water rushes from the reservoir down through the penstocks to the hydroelectric power station at the base of the dam.

Reservoir
A reservoir is a deep lake that is created when the flow of a river is dammed up. The lake fills part of the valley where the river flows. A reservoir can be hundreds of kilometers (miles) long.

Screens
These are covers at the entrance of the penstocks to keep out fish, twigs and dirt.

48

So that the water can be used to generate a lot of electricity.

One Way to Become Famous

Create an experiment that answers Riley's question and can be used during the debate.

- Cut a rectangle 2.5 cm × 5 cm (1 in. × 2 in.) out of a plastic lid.
- Turn on the cold water full blast in the kitchen sink. (Make sure the drain is open.)
- Hold the rectangle right under the faucet, and let the water run onto its tip.
- Then hold the rectangle near the bottom of the sink and let the water run onto its tip.

The water near the bottom of the sink bends the plastic rectangle, while the water under the faucet hardly moves it. That's because the farther water falls, the more force it has. In a hydroelectric power station, the greater the force of the water, the more power the station can produce. Dams must be tall and reservoirs must be deep to create a great force of falling water.

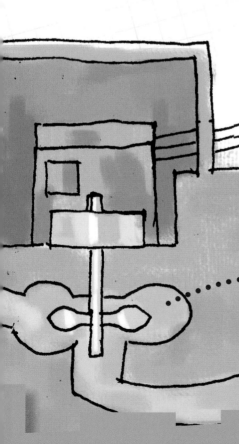

Turbine propeller
This goes inside the power station of the hydroelectric plant. It is spun by the water falling down from the reservoir. The turbine is connected to a generator that produces electricity.

More Dam Info

As far as I can tell, there are four main types of dams — embankment, arch, buttress and gravity dams. They have different shapes and are made of different materials, but they all block the flow of water in a river.

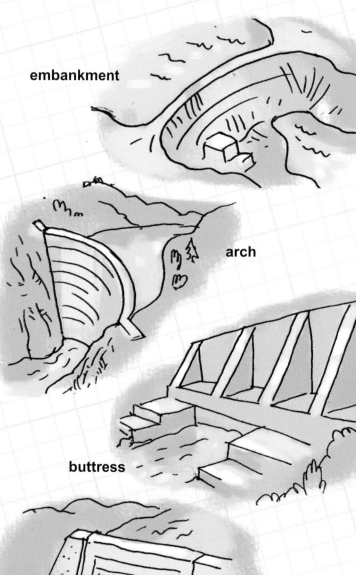

embankment

arch

buttress

gravity dams

Itá Dam

Location: on the Uruguay River in Brazil

Purpose: to produce hydroelectricity

Type: embankment dam (built in wide valleys)

Height: 120 m (400 ft.) — as tall as a forty-story skyscraper

Materials: millions of tons of rock, sand, earth and clay squashed together with heavy rollers and then covered with concrete to make it watertight

Strength: The dam gets its strength from its triangular shape and from its weight.

Daniel-Johnson Dam

Location: on the Manicouagan River in Canada

Purpose: to produce hydroelectricity

Type: multiple arch and buttress dam (built in wide, flat river valleys)

Height: 214 m (700 ft.) — as tall as a seventy-story skyscraper

Materials: reinforced concrete

Strength: Triangular-shaped wedges called buttresses push against the dam wall and the force of the reservoir's water. Arches join the buttresses and strengthen them.

Three Gorges Dam

Location: on the Yangtze River in China

Purpose: to produce hydroelectricity, control floods and increase shipping

Type: gravity dam (built in wide, flat river valleys)

Height: 185 m (605 ft.) — as tall as a sixty-story skyscraper

Materials: concrete

Strength: The dam's tremendous weight stops the reservoir's water from pushing it over. It is much thicker at the bottom than at the top.

This way to the arch dam!

Kariba Dam

Location: on the Zambezi River between Zambia and Zimbabwe

Purpose: to produce hydroelectricity

Type: arch dam (built in narrow rocky canyons)

Height: 130 m (425 ft.) — as tall as a forty-two-story skyscraper

Materials: reinforced concrete

Strength: The dam gets its strength from its arch shape. The rocky, steep sides of the canyon act as supporting abutments. (That's just like an arch bridge!)

Check This Out

Dad says that the reason dams are so much thicker at the bottom is because more water pressure is pushing against the bottom part. That didn't make sense to me, so Dad said to try this:

- Find an empty 2 L (2 qt.) milk or juice container. Open its top.
- With a skewer or a small nail, punch three holes — one near the bottom, one in the middle and one near the top.
- Stand the container on the edge of the sink. Fill it with water from a jug.
- Watch how far the water squirts from each hole.

Dad says that the water coming out of the bottom hole will reach the farthest because the water at the bottom is under more pressure. (Maybe I can use this as a demo during my debate.)

To Dam or Not to Dam

Hey, this could be a good beginning for your speech!

Pros

• The power stations of dams can produce hydroelectricity for millions of people. Hydroelectricity is a renewable source of energy since rainfall renews the water in the reservoir.

• Hydro-electrical power stations can replace coal-burning power stations which produce greenhouse gases.

• Heavy rainstorms or spring snowmelts can cause the banks of a river to overflow, damaging crops and homes. Some dams are built to manage floods by controlling the amount of water entering a river.

• The reservoirs of dams can help farmers water their crops and animals, even during dry seasons. Water flows from the reservoir through pipes and canals to farmers' fields.

• The building of a dam creates jobs. People are employed to build and operate the dam. As well, lakes formed by dams often increase tourism which helps the economy of an area.

Cons

• Lakes created by dams can bring more tourists to natural areas. This means an increase in car exhaust, water and electricity use, garbage and sewage.

• People who live in valleys behind dams can lose their homes when reservoirs are created. Valuable artifacts and sacred sites might also disappear.

• Ecosystems including plants, animals, insects and birds can disappear when valleys are flooded.

• Some dams make it difficult for salmon and other fish to migrate despite the building of fish ladders.

• Water flowing downstream from a dam is often very cold because it comes from the lower part of the reservoir, where there is little sunlight. This cold water changes fish and insect habitats.

Tomorrow I find out which side I'm defending. It's about time!

53

Dikes

Darn it! I got the pro side. I was so wishing for the con side. When Mr. Evans saw my gloomy face, he suggested that I research dikes. He said that a dike is a kind of dam, but instead of keeping water in, it keeps water out. He said that dikes have a lot going for them. More research, ugh. Still, if it helps me win the debate ... At least Mr. Evans gave me some photos and names "to investigate."

The Afsluitdijk

The "dijk" part of this name is the Dutch word for dike. Mr. Evans was right. This dike is really amazing. It's more than four car lanes wide, runs 32 km (20 mi.) over water and joins two pieces of land — but it's not a bridge. It's a wall built out of millions of cubic meters (yards) of sand and clay. It stands on the bottom of the North Sea and was built to stop the North Sea from flooding the low-lying Netherlands.

The Afsluitdijk enclosed a huge bay, which then became a lake. Within this lake, other dikes were built to enclose smaller areas of water. The water was then pumped out, leaving new pieces of land, called polders. Polders have both farms and towns on them. The building of these dikes actually increased the size of the Netherlands!

The Bay of Fundy Dikes

I never knew that Canada had dikes and that they were originally built over 350 years ago! They're not as huge as the dikes in the Netherlands, but considering that the Acadians (French settlers) used only horses, oxen and simple hand tools to build them, they're pretty impressive. The dikes were built to stop the high tides of the Bay of Fundy from entering the salt marshes along its coast. They were built with small trees, mud and grass. The Acadians drained the salt water out of the marshes and planted crops in the nutrient-rich soil.

While there are lots of dikes still standing along the Bay of Fundy today, not all dike lands are used for farming. Some of them support a lot of wildlife, such as beavers, muskrat, red fox, deer, coyotes, fish and insects. The Bay of Fundy dike lands are also on the migration route of many bird species. More pros for dams (well, really, dikes)!

The Thames Barrier

This is some crazy barrier. It has nine piers that are larger than two tennis courts laid end to end. The stainless steel roofs of the piers protect machinery inside the piers. The machinery operates the gates that block the Thames River during storm surges. Six of the gates rise up from the riverbed, and four gates near the banks of the river lower into the water. It takes one-and-a-half hours for all of the gates to close off the river. One hundred people work at the Thames Barrier (a good source of employment and an additional point for the pro side!).

The Maeslant Barrier

This is another flood barrier to protect the Netherlands, but this one moves! It closes when a storm surge is heading toward the port of Rotterdam. (A surge happens when a storm and high tide come at the same time.) A computer system senses the surge coming and sets two humongous hollow steel gates in motion. (Each gate is almost as long as two football fields laid end to end!) The gates swing toward each other, and when they meet, they fill with water. The weight of the water sinks them to the bottom of the waterway. When the storm is over, the gates empty, float to the surface and open to let ships pass through. How awesome is that?!

The Maeslant Barrier is really cool, but will it help your argument?

Absolutely. In 1953, floods killed 1800 people in the Netherlands. The Maeslant Barrier will stop this from ever happening again.

Locks

Our class trip to Ottawa isn't even over and we already have another assignment. We have to write an account of our favorite part of the trip and "it must be done in a creative manner."

No contest. Other than eating the best sushi ever (but I can't write about that), the best part was the tour of the locks on the Rideau Canal.

The Locks of the Rideau Canal by Corry Lapont

On Tuesday, May 25, 2011, after a tour of the Parliament Buildings, my class and I walked down to a set of eight locks on the Rideau Canal.

The Rideau Canal is a series of rivers and lakes connected by canals, which are channels of water that people have dug out.

Along the canals are 47 locks. The canals and locks allow boats to get around rapids and waterfalls.

In Ottawa there is a drop of 24 m (80 ft.) between the channel of the Rideau Canal and the Ottawa River. The set of eight locks allows boats to travel from the canal to the river and back. The locks also act like a dam slowing the water down.

24m (80ft.)

There's a boat going into the first lock.

Yes. It's "locking down," which means it's going downstream. Notice the water level in the lock. It's at the same level as the water in the channel.

Levees

64 Parkwood Drive,
Daly City, California
June 6, 2010

Dear Corry,

It was great to hear from you, even if it's only to pick my brain about levees. (Just kidding!) Yes, you're right. A levee is a kind of dam. A levee is usually a small embankment dam built out of earth and covered with grass. (See photo.) It runs along the sides of canals and rivers to prevent flooding.

Your mom is right, too. I do know a lot about levees. I'm an engineer who tries to figure out why a certain levee has failed. So I'm not sure that I can provide many pro arguments for your debate. However, I can tell you how a levee can be constructed to protect land from flooding.

Although I've investigated many levees in Europe, the ones I found most interesting were the levees in New Orleans, Louisiana. As you probably know, several New Orleans levees failed during Hurricane Katrina in 2005. There were many reasons for these failures. Out of fear of boring you, I'll list just a few.

First of all, I need to explain that the levees in New Orleans have flood walls running along the tops of them. The flood walls are concrete walls built with sheets of steel called sheet pilings. One end of the sheet piling is embedded in the concrete, and the other end goes into the ground. (See Diagram 1.)

Unfortunately, the sheet pilings weren't made tall enough to support the walls. They should have been embedded in clay, which is solid, gives more support and is found deeper in the ground. Instead, the sheet pilings were embedded in sand or soft marshy soil. The sheet pilings couldn't stop the storm surge water from pushing over the wall.

Levee

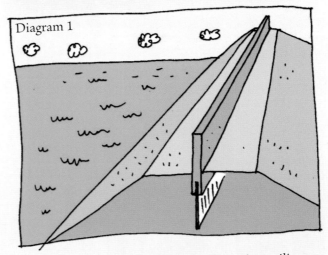
Diagram 1

Another thing that happened was that water seeped from the canal through the sand under the sheet pilings and up the other side. In a very short time, an underground channel formed, allowing tons of water and sand to flood the land. This weakened the wall, causing it to collapse. (See diagrams 2 and 3.)

The flood walls that collapsed are called I-walls. They stood straight up and down in the earth of the levee. When water overtopped (came over the top) some of the levees, the water eroded the soil at the base of the wall. The weakened earth could no longer support the wall, and the wall fell over. (See photo.)

So, how do we build levees that will resist future hurricanes?

1. Make sure that sheet pilings are longer and embedded in clay.

2. Build flood walls like an upside-down T. (They're called T-walls. See Diagram 4.) Concrete at the base of the wall stops overtopping water from eroding the earth.

3. Embed sensors in the walls, like they do in the Netherlands. The sensors monitor ongoing structural changes that might be weakening the walls.

4. Build flood barrier gates and pumps to stop water from entering canals and rivers. (They built these in New Orleans after Katrina.)

Well, Corry, I guess I have given you a pro argument after all. Levees can be effective if they're constructed properly. Good luck with your debate. Let me know what happens.

Your favorite uncle,

George

Uncle George

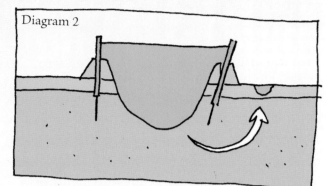
Diagram 2

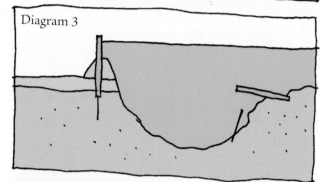
Diagram 3

Overtopped Floodwall

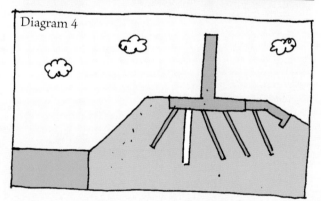
Diagram 4

Making Plans

There are so many interesting structures I want to see up close and personal. I need another scrapbook just to keep track of them all. Too bad this one's full. I'll still keep an eye on all the new and environmentally friendly structures people are building, but in the meantime, I can visit the awesome and unusual ones already built, especially those that are still standing after hundreds of years!

The Laerdal Tunnel
What I really want to see in this Norwegian tunnel are the three caverns along the route. They're lit to represent a sunrise.

The Turning Torso
This Swedish skyscraper is so weird but so cool. It's supposed to represent a twisting body.

The Hoover Dam
You can walk across the top of this dam in the U.S. — one of the largest in the world!

The Duomo

I can't wait to climb to the top of this six-hundred-year-old dome in Italy. I want to see how Brunelleschi built it without scaffolding and without modern machinery.

The Rolling Bridge

This is pure genius! It looks like a simple beam bridge. But when boats come along, this bridge curls up to form an octagon at the side of the canal. I hope I can go to the U.K. to see it happen.

What I Want to Be

Why do adults always ask the same questions? "What are you going to be when you grow up? Are you going to follow in your parents' footsteps?" How am I supposed to know? I don't have a crystal ball.

I might be a designer or an architect or an engineer or an urban planner. Actually, it would be really cool to work in a place like the Heatherwick Studio in London, England. Dad says that the owner, Thomas Heatherwick, is the man who designed the Rolling Bridge and that he works with a whole team of architects and engineers on all kinds of amazing structures. Hmm … I wonder if I could be a designer, architect and engineer all at the same time. The one thing I am sure about is that whatever I design or plan or build, it will be green.

Corry Lapont

Glossary

abutments: supports at the ends of a bridge

anchorages: concrete blocks which hold the ends of the cables of a suspension bridge

architect: a person who designs buildings

beam: a length of wood or metal that stretches across a gap

bedrock: solid rock that lies beneath the surface of the earth

cables: thick steel ropes that support the roadway of a suspension bridge

canal: an artificial waterway

civil engineer: an engineer who plans and directs the building of bridges, roads, dams, canals and buildings

cladding: material used for the outside of a building

cofferdam: a large structure used to keep water out of an underwater area

column: a length of wood or metal that stands upright to help support a structure

compression: a stress on an object caused by pushing or squeezing

core: a vertical tube-like structure that helps support a skyscraper

cross-bracing: large steel Xs on a skyscraper that give it strength

dam: a large heavy wall built to hold back flowing water

damper: a large heavy object used to reduce the sway of a skyscraper in high winds

deck: the roadway of a bridge

dike: a barrier of earth built to prevent flooding

ecosystem: a habitat in which the soil, plants and animals function interdependently

façade: the outer wall of a building

foundation: the part of a building below ground that supports the rest of the building

geotechnical engineer: an engineer who checks the underground before a structure is built

geothermal: heat energy that comes from deep inside the earth

green design: environmentally friendly design

Everything you design is going to be green? That's so-o-o boring.

Riley, green means ...

hydroelectricity: electricity produced by falling water

levee: a barrier built to prevent flooding

load: weight on a structure

lock: a section of a canal that allows boats to go from one level of water to another

pier: a support of a bridge

recycle: to reuse the material of objects for another purpose

reinforced concrete: concrete with steel rods running through it to increase the strength of the concrete

reservoir: a lake formed when a dam is built

solar cells: a device that uses sunlight to make electricity

span: a section of a bridge between two supports

spillway: a channel on a dam used for the escape of excess water

TBM: Tunnel Boring Machine — a large machine used to dig tunnels

tension: a stress on an object caused by pulling

torsion: a twisting movement

typhoon: a tropical hurricane that happens in the Pacific and Indian Oceans

urban planner: a person who plans the growth of a city

I was just kidding. Green means using low energy lights and natural light; using renewable power sources like solar, wind or geothermal; using recycled materials for building and recycling building wastes; using rainwater instead of city water; using sustainable materials; lessening a building's impact on the environment and so on and so on.

Wow. I'm impressed. How do you know all that?

I've been reading your scrapbook!

Index